GIANNIS ANTETOKOUNMPO
Making a Difference Through Basketball

By Katie Kawa

KidHaven
PUBLISHING

People Who Make a Difference

Published in 2025 by
KidHaven Publishing, an Imprint of Greenhaven Publishing, LLC
2544 Clinton St.
Buffalo, NY 14224

Designer: Deanna Lepovich
Editor: Katie Kawa

Photo credits: Cover SOPA Images Limited/Alamy Stock Photo; p. 5 Xinhua/Alamy Stock Photo; p. 6 Minaeva Emma/Shutterstock.com; p. 7, 19, 20 Sipa USA/Alamy Stock Photo; pp. 9, 15 Ververidis Vasilis/Shutterstock.com; p. 11 Marty Jean-Louis/Alamy Stock Photo; p. 13 White House Photo/Alamy Stock Photo; p. 17 Greek photonews/Alamy Stock Photo; p. 21 T.Sumaetho/Shutterstock.com.

Library of Congress Cataloging-in-Publication Data

Names: Kawa, Katie, author.
Title: Giannis Antetokounmpo : making a difference through basketball /
    Katie Kawa.
Description: First. | Buffalo, New York : KidHaven Publishing, [2025] |
    Series: People who make a difference | Includes index.
Identifiers: LCCN 2024006336 | ISBN 9781534548077 (library binding) | ISBN
    9781534548060 (paperback) | ISBN 9781534548084 (ebook)
Subjects: LCSH: Antetokounmpo, Giannis, 1994—Juvenile literature. |
    Centers (Basketball)–Greece–Biography–Juvenile literature. |
    Basketball players–United States–Juvenile literature. | Milwaukee
    Bucks (Basketball team)–Juvenile literature. | National Basketball
    Association–Juvenile literature. | African American
    philanthropists–Juvenile literature.
Classification: LCC GV884.A56 K39 2025 | DDC 796.323092

Printed in the United States of America

Some of the images in this book illustrate individuals who are models. The depictions do not imply actual situations or events.

CPSIA compliance information: Batch #CSKH25: For further information contact Greenhaven Publishing LLC at 1-844-317-7404.

Please visit our website, www.greenhavenpublishing.com. For a free color catalog of all our high-quality books, call toll free 1-844-317-7404 or fax 1-844-317-7405.

Find us on

CONTENTS

A SURPRISING PATH

Every person follows their own path to become who they're meant to be. For some people, that path is full of twists, turns, and surprises. That's certainly been true for Giannis Antetokounmpo. His path took him from a hard childhood in Greece to basketball superstardom in the United States!

Giannis has found success, but he hasn't forgotten the struggles he faced along the way. In fact, he works hard to give back to people who are facing their own struggles. His story has **inspired** many people to believe that anyone can make a difference—no matter where they come from.

In His Words

"It's a kid living his dream and it's also a kid still trying to figure out all of the things that happen because of it. I'm just like everybody else, I'm trying to navigate [figure out] life."

— Interview with *Esquire* magazine from October 2022

Giannis Antetokounmpo has found fame playing for the Milwaukee Bucks in the National Basketball Association (NBA). Milwaukee, Wisconsin, became his home when he first started playing there, and he's found many ways to make a difference in this city.

NOT AN EASY CHILDHOOD

Giannis's story began an ocean away from Milwaukee. He was born on December 6, 1994, in Athens, Greece. His parents, Charles and Veronica, came to Greece from Nigeria. They tried to find work in Athens while raising Giannis and his brothers, but it wasn't easy.

Charles and Veronica lived in fear that they would be deported, or sent back to Nigeria. They had very little money, and Giannis did what he could to help his parents. Sometimes this meant selling items on the streets of Athens to tourists, or visitors.

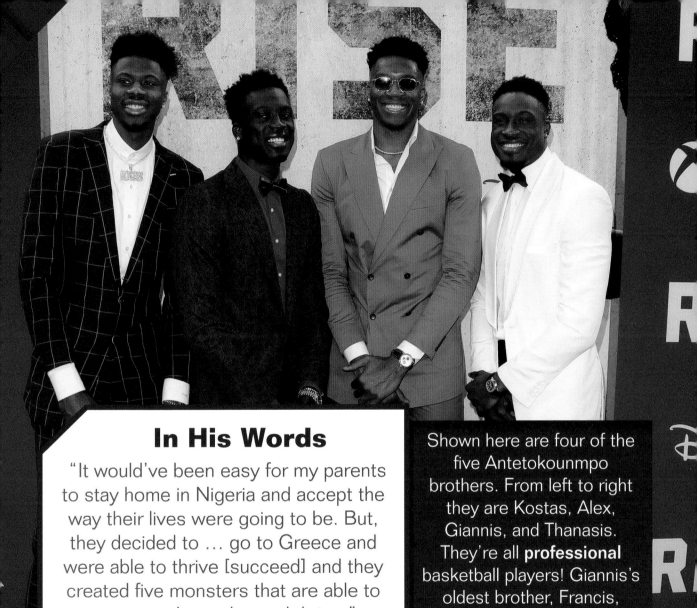

In His Words

"It would've been easy for my parents to stay home in Nigeria and accept the way their lives were going to be. But, they decided to … go to Greece and were able to thrive [succeed] and they created five monsters that are able to go somewhere else and thrive."

— Interview with *Esquire* magazine from October 2022

Shown here are four of the five Antetokounmpo brothers. From left to right they are Kostas, Alex, Giannis, and Thanasis. They're all **professional** basketball players! Giannis's oldest brother, Francis, played professional soccer and is a musician.

BECOMING A BALLER

Giannis didn't grow up with dreams of being a basketball player. However, a coach in Athens saw him running around with his friends and believed that's exactly what he could grow up to be. After playing on youth teams for a few years, Giannis joined the senior, or oldest, team of the Greek basketball club known as Filathlitikos in 2011.

Giannis's skills and size caught the attention of NBA scouts—people whose job it is to find the best players. In 2013, he was drafted, or chosen, to play for the Milwaukee Bucks.

In His Words

"I can't push it [my past in Greece] to the side … I can't say, 'I've made it, I'm done with all that.' I will always carry it with me. It's where I learned to work like this."

— Interview for *TIME* magazine's "American Voices 2017"

Giannis didn't start playing basketball until he was 13 years old, but his height helped him find success on the court. Giannis is almost 7 feet (2 m) tall!

MOST IMPROVED

Giannis moved from Greece to the United States so he could start his NBA **career**. He played his first game for the Bucks in October 2013, but he didn't find success right away. In Giannis's first season, the Bucks only won 15 games and lost 67, which was the worst record in the NBA that season.

The next season, Giannis improved as a player, and the Bucks improved as a team. They made it to the NBA **playoffs** in 2015 and again in 2017. That year, Giannis was named the NBA's Most Improved Player!

In His Words

"There's no failure in sports. There's good days, bad days. Some days you're able to be successful; some days you're not. Some days it's your turn; some days it's not your turn. And that's what sports is about. You don't always win."

— Press conference after losing in the playoffs in April 2023

The last name on the back of Giannis's Bucks jersey is Antetokounmpo. However, he was born with the last name Adetokunbo. When he became a Greek citizen before moving to the United States, his last name needed to be spelled using the Greek alphabet. This meant Adetokunbo, which is Nigerian, became Antetokounmpo.

THE MVP

Giannis's star continued to rise, and the Bucks continued to find success. In 2019, he was named the NBA's Most **Valuable** Player (MVP). The next year, he was named MVP again and was also named the NBA's Defensive Player of the Year. This honor is given to the player who's the best at keeping the other team from scoring.

In 2021, Giannis led the Bucks to a **championship** when they beat the Phoenix Suns in the NBA Finals. Giannis was named the Finals MVP, which meant he was the best player in the Finals.

In His Words

"In order for you to be the best, you have to play like the best. You have to practice like the best. You [have] to carry yourself like the best. Which is not easy."

— Interview with the *Milwaukee Journal Sentinel* from April 2023

Giannis wasn't the only member of the Antetokounmpo family to win a championship with the Bucks in 2021. His brother Thanasis was also on the team! They're shown here visiting President Joe Biden after winning the championship.

THE GREEK FREAK

The Bucks made it to the NBA playoffs again in 2022 and 2023. Although they didn't win a championship in those years, Giannis continued to make big plays and stay in the spotlight. In November 2023, Giannis became the youngest player in NBA history to record at least 16,000 points, 17,000 **rebounds**, and 3,000 **assists** in their career.

Giannis has also stayed in the spotlight in Greece. He began playing for the country's national team in 2013. As a member of the national team, he plays against players from other countries in international tournaments, or sets of games.

In His Words

"I believe that being an **immigrant** helps you become stronger."

— Interview with *Esquire* magazine from October 2022

Giannis's size and skills have earned him the nickname the Greek Freak because there's no other player like him!

GIVING BACK

Giannis knows that playing in the NBA has given him the fame and the money to help others and support causes that matter to him. In 2022, he and his family decided to give back to others in a big way by starting the Charles Antetokounmpo Family Foundation (CAFF).

This foundation allows Giannis, his brothers, and their mother to support many different causes they care about. This includes helping immigrants, creating better educational opportunities for kids, and helping women whose husbands have died. CAFF works in the places this family has called home—Nigeria, Greece, and the United States.

In His Words

"We decided as a family to come together and build this foundation to … do what people did for us … Put our hand out there and give them an opportunity … to go out there and accomplish their dreams the same way I did."

— Interview on *The Daily Show* from February 2023

Giannis and his family (including his mother and brother Alex, who are shown here) named their foundation in honor of Charles Antetokounmpo, who died in 2017.

MENTAL HEALTH HELP

One of the causes that means the most to Giannis is **mental** health. He's been open about talking to a mental health professional to help him through the hard times that have come with moving to a new country and playing in the NBA. He wants to show others, especially other men, that talking about your feelings and taking care of your mental health is important.

In 2023, Giannis donated $1 million to support mental health services in Milwaukee. This helped provide free mental health care for people in the city.

In His Words

"I gave it a chance. I started talking with someone … Somebody helped put me in a place, again, to … be OK with myself. To—no matter what the **outcome** is of the game—understand that I can't control that. I can only control my effort. How hard I work. How I make people feel around me. How I try to, hopefully, inspire people from what I do."

— Interview with the *Milwaukee Journal Sentinel* from April 2023

The Life of
Giannis Antetokounmpo

1994
Giannis is born in Greece on December 6.

2011
Giannis joins the senior Filathlitikos basketball team.

2013
Giannis is drafted by the Milwaukee Bucks and plays in his first NBA game.

2015
Giannis plays in the NBA playoffs for the first time.

2017
Giannis is named the NBA's Most Improved Player.

2019
Giannis is named the NBA's MVP.

2020
Giannis's son Liam is born in February, and Giannis is named the NBA's Defensive Player of the Year, in addition to being named MVP again.

2021
The Bucks win the NBA championship, Giannis is named Finals MVP, and his son Maverick is born in August.

2022
Giannis and his family start the Charles Antetokounmpo Family Foundation, and the movie *Rise*, which tells his family's story, comes out on Disney+.

2023
Giannis donates $1 million to mental health services in Milwaukee, and his daughter Eva is born in September.

2024
The **documentary** *Giannis: The Marvelous Journey* comes out in February.

Giannis's life has been filled with inspiring moments.

AN INSPIRING STORY

Giannis's story is so inspiring that it's been made into a movie—twice! In 2022, the movie *Rise* came out on Disney+. It tells the story of the whole Antetokounmpo family. Then, in 2024, *Giannis: The Marvelous Journey* came out on Amazon Prime. Unlike *Rise*, this movie is a documentary.

Giannis's strong connection with his family is a part of these movies, and his family has grown over the years. As of 2024, he has two sons and a daughter. Being a good dad is just one more way Giannis Antetokounmpo makes a difference in the world around him.

In His Words

"This is just the beginning … As my dad told me … always want more but never be greedy."

— Speech after being named NBA MVP in 2019

Be Like Giannis Antetokounmpo!

Remind the people in your life that it's good to care for their mental health.

Raise money for groups that help immigrants in your community.

Help your family members around the house by doing things such as picking up your toys, cleaning your room, setting the table, and other chores.

If you know any immigrants, treat them with respect and kindness.

Practice and work hard to improve your skills—in school, sports, music, and more!

Share your feeliings with people you trust instead of pushing them down. If you feel like you need extra help, ask to talk with a mental health professional.

You don't have to be a superstar basketball player to be like Giannis Antetokounmpo. You can find your own ways to help your family, your community, and yourself!

GLOSSARY

assist: An action by one player that allows their teammate to score in a game of basketball.

career: A period of time spent doing a job or activity.

championship: A contest to find out who's the best player or team in a sport.

documentary: A nonfiction movie or television program presenting facts about a topic.

immigrant: A person who comes to a country to live there.

inspire: To move someone to do something great.

mental: Relating to the mind.

outcome: Something that follows as a result.

playoffs: A series of games played after the regular season of a sport is over to find out who the best team is that season.

professional: Having to do with a job someone does for a living. Also, a person who does a job that requires special education or skill.

rebound: The act of getting control of the basketball after a missed shot.

valuable: Having great worth or importance.

FOR MORE INFORMATION

WEBSITES

Charles Antetokounmpo Family Foundation

caff.foundation

CAFF's website explains the work the foundation does.

NBA.com: Giannis Antetokounmpo

www.nba.com/player/203507/giannis-antetokounmpo

Visit the official NBA website for facts about Giannis's professional career, as well as videos and news stories about him.

BOOKS

Gardiner, Nora. *Giannis Antetokounmpo*. Buffalo, NY: Enslow Publishing, 2022.

Morey, Allan. *Giannis Antetokounmpo*. Minneapolis, MN: Bellwether Media, 2023.

Stabler, David. *Meet Giannis Antetokounmpo*. Minneapolis, MN: Lerner Publications, 2023.

INDEX